MASTER YOUR EMOTIONS & MOTIVATION

---

2 BOOKS IN 1

THIBAUT MEURISSE

How to use this workbook

This workbook is to be used together with the book "Master Your Emotions & Motivation: 2 Books in 1".

If you haven't grabbed the boxset, you can get it at the URL below:

http://mybook.to/boxset1

I encourage you to complete all the exercises in this workbook. The more effort you put into it, the better results you'll get and the better you'll feel about yourself.

Let's get started, shall we?

MASTER YOUR EMOTIONS WORKBOOK

1

———

PART I. WHAT EMOTIONS ARE

Have you ever wondered what emotions are and what purpose they serve?

In this section, we'll discuss how your survival mechanism affects your emotions. Then, we'll explain what the 'ego' is and how it impacts your emotions. Finally, we'll discover the mechanism behind emotions and learn why negative emotions can be so hard to deal with.

1. Bias towards negativity

Find one example of an imaginary threat resulting from your survival mechanism. Can you see how the mind works? Feel free to write down your example below:

2. Happiness

Identify things that you believe give you shots of dopamine (TV, video games, gambling, social media etc.) . Write them down:

-

-

-

-

-

-

-

Which one of these things are you the most 'addicted' to. What activity, if you were to take a break from, would you be craving? Write it down:

____

____

____

____

3. The nature of the ego

Write down the things you feel you identify the most with (your body, your relationships, your country, your religion, your car etc.)

-

-

-

-

-

-

-

-

-

-

-

On a scale of 0 to 10 how true are the following statements?

My ego tends to equate having with being

0   10

My ego lives through comparison

0   10

My ego is never satisfied

0   10

My ego needs other people's approval to feel valued

0   10

I enhance my value by trying to associate with smart or famous people

0   10

I like to gossip

0   10

I have an inferiority complex

0 ____ 10

I have a superiority complex

0 ____ 10

I look for fame

0 ____ 10

I constantly try to be right

0 ____ 10

I often complain

0 ____ 10

I seek attention (recognition, praise or admiration)

0 ____ 10

How does your ego impact your emotions? Write down some of
the ways your ego generates negative emotions. Try to be specific.

____

____

____

____

____

What could you do about it?

____

____

____

____

____

4. The nature of emotions

To help you understand the nature of emotions, we'll focus on just one specific emotion in this section.

Take just a few minutes to go through the following 10 steps by visualizing each step in your mind and answering the questions below. If it helps, you can close your eyes.

Step 1. Select one negative emotion you experienced recently.

My negative emotion:

Step 2. Acknowledge that this emotion isn't bad. See how it comes and goes and isn't you.

Step 3. Remember that emotion and notice how it is nowhere to be found in your present reality.

Step 4. Ask yourself what you can learn from that emotion. What is it trying to tell you and how can you use it to grow?

Write down your answer below:

____

____

____

____

Step 5. Notice how that negative emotion tainted all your experiences, perhaps, even tricking you to believe you'll never get out it.

Write down below how it distorted your thinking (ex: made you feel stuck, made you believe you'll never be happy again etc.):

____

____

____

____

Step 6. Remember how you felt the need to identify with this negative emotion and/or with the story that goes with it. Then, entertain the idea that you could have detached yourself from it.

Step 7. Remember how this negative emotion seemed to narrow down your perspective. Write down how below:

____

____

____

____

Step 8. See how you were attracting more negative emotions. Write down below the negative emotions you were attracting:

____

____

____

____

Step 9. Notice how you created mental suffering out of that emotion by adding your own judgment to it. Write down the interpretation you added to that emotion:

____

____

____

____

Step 10. Finally, realize that your negative emotion exists only in your mind and notice that reality has no problem.

2

PART II. WHAT IMPACTS YOUR EMOTIONS

> Your mind operates on the famous computing principle of GIGO - garbage in, garbage out. If you do ill, speak ill and think ill, the residue is going to leave you sick. If you do well, speak well and think well, the outcome is going to be well.

— OM SWAMI, A MILLION THOUGHTS.

Emotions are complex, and a variety of factors influence how you feel. In this section, we'll cover some of the elements affecting what drives your emotions. The good news is, you have some control over them.

If we exclude spontaneous emotional reactions resulting from your survival mechanism, most of your emotions are self-created. They result from the way you interpret thoughts or events. However, these aren't the only elements that affect your emotional state. Your body, your voice, the food you eat, or how much your sleep, also play a role in determining the quality of your emotions and therefore the quality of your life.

Let's see how each of these elements impact your emotions. To start changing your emotions positively, make sure you complete the exercises below.

1. How will you use your body?

What type of exercising will you do? Will you use power posture? (for an example of power posture search for "TED talk Amy Cuddy" on YouTube). Write down your answers below:

____

____

____

____

2. How will you use your thoughts?

Will you meditate, use positive affirmations or visualization?

Examples:

- I will visualize my goal every morning for 5 minutes allowing myself to feel as if I had already accomplished it
- I will meditate 5 minutes every day for 30 days as soon as I wake up
- I will repeat the affirmation "I love being confident" for 5 minutes every day

Write down one thing you will do to better use your thoughts and positively affect the way you feel:

____

____

____

____

3. How will you improve your sleep?

Examples:

- I will meditate before going to bed
- I will create a 10 minutes evening ritual including gratitude exercises, stretching, and meditation

Write down below one thing you could do to improve your sleep:

____

____

____

____

4. How will you use your breathing?

Example: each time I feel some negative emotions, I will breathe slowly for a few minutes

Write down below one thing you could use breathing to improve your mood:

____

____

____

____

5. How changing your environment could improve your emotions?

Examples:

- I will read inspirational books for 15 minutes each day and cut off the time I spend watching TV
- I will spend less time with negative friends
- I will spend only 15 minutes on social media each day for 30 days

Write down below one thing you could do to improve your environment:

____

____

____

____

6. How will you use music to improve your mood?

Examples:

- I will listen to gratitude songs while doing my gratitude exercises each morning
- I will listen to/ watch motivational videos when I start feeling a little bit down and dance or move my body to change my emotional state
- I will listen to classical music or white noise to better focus when I work

Write down below one way you could use music to improve your mood:

____

____

____

____

3

PART III. HOW TO CHANGE YOUR EMOTIONS

> The mind always seeks to deny the Now and to escape from it. In other words, the more you are identified with your mind, the more you suffer. Or you may put it like this: the more you are able to honor and accept the Now, the more you are free of pain, of suffering—and free of the egoic mind.
>
> — ECKHART TOLLE, THE POWER OF NOW.

In this section, we'll explore how you can deal with negative emotions and condition your mind to experience more positive ones.

Make sure you complete the exercises in this section to help you:

* Let go of your emotions
* Change your story and create a more empowering one
* Condition your mind
* Use your behaviors to change your emotions, and
* Modify your environment to reduce negative emotions.

Let's get started.

How emotions are formed

As mentioned in the book, emotions are formed as follows:

Interpretation + identification + repetition = strong emotion

* **Interpretation:** When you interpret an event or a thought based on your personal story.
* **Identification:** When you identify with a specific thought as it arises.
* **Repetition:** It is having the same thoughts over and over.
* **Strong emotion:** When you experience an emotion so many times that it has become part of your identity. You then experience that emotion whenever related thoughts or events trigger it.

Revisiting past events

Remember a past event when you experience negative emotions. It could be the last time you were depressed, sad, angry or felt like you weren't good enough.

Now, write down what happens for each of the following:

Interpretation: What events happen and what thoughts arose?

____

____

____

____

Identification: How you respond to these thoughts?

____

____

____

____

Repetition: Did you identify with these thoughts repeatedly?

____

____

____

____

Changing your story

Analyze your story by answering the questions below:

One or two emotional issues you currently have. Ask yourself, "What emotions if I could get rid of, would have the most positive impact on my life?"

____

____

____

____

Your interpretation of these issues. Ask yourself, "What would I need to believe for my story to be true?"

____

____

____

____

New empowering meanings. Ask yourself, "What would I need to believe to avoid experiencing these negative emotions?"

____

____

____

____

Letting go of your emotions

Make a list of the emotions you would like to let go of.

Perhaps, you feel like you aren't good enough. Or you struggle with procrastination. Or maybe you blame yourself for something you did in the past. Just write down whatever comes to your mind.

-

-

-

-

-

-

-

-

Select one emotion then ask yourself:

- "Could I let this feeling go?"
- "Would I"? (Yes/no)
- "When?" (NOW)

The emotion I want to let go of:

____

____

____

____

Conditioning your mind

Get into the habit of depositing positive thoughts in your mind every day. Choose one emotion you want to experience more of in your life and commit to conditioning your mind every day for at least 30 days.

Examples of emotions:

- Gratitude
- Excitement
- Self-esteem
- Certainty
- Decisiveness

My emotion(s):

____

____

____

____

How exactly I will condition my mind (example: I will close my eyes and say "thank you" to all people that cross my mind while acknowledging one good thing they did for me.

____

____

____

____

Changing your emotions by changing your behaviors

Remember the last time you experience a negative emotion that lasted for a couple of days or more. Write it down below:

____

____

____

____

Now, write down what you did specifically to overcome that negative emotion:

____

____

____

____

Then, ask yourself, "How could I have changed my behavior in such a way that it would have influenced my emotions positively?". Write it down below:

____

____

____

____

Changing your environment

Write down below any activities that you believe may negatively impact your emotions. (Examples: Negative friends, TV, gossiping, social media, video games etc.). Then, next to each activity write down what are the consequences (It makes you feel guilty, demotivates you, erodes your self-esteem etc.)

Activities	Consequences

Write down what you could instead that you improve your mood:

____

____

____

____

____

Short-term and long-term solutions to deal with negative emotions

> No other life-form on the planet knows negativity, only humans, just as no other life-form violates and poisons the Earth that sustains it. Have you ever seen an unhappy flower or a stressed oak tree? Have you come across a depressed dolphin, a frog that has a problem with self-esteem, a cat that cannot relax, or a bird that carries hatred and resentment? The only animals that may occasionally experience something akin to negativity or show signs of neurotic behavior are those that live in close contact with humans and so link into the human mind and its insanity.
>
> — ECKHART TOLLE, THE POWER OF NOW.

In this section, I will provide you with a list of exercises or techniques you can use to better deal with negative emotions. No matter how much control you have over your mind, you'll still experience a whole bunch of negative emotions in the future, from mild frustration to depression. You'd better be prepared.

I've listed below some things you can do to deal with negative emotions and have included both long-term and short-term solutions.

1. Short-term solutions

The following techniques will help you manage negative emotions as they arise. Try them out, and keep the ones that work for you.

A. Change your emotional state

- **Distract yourself:** An emotion is only as strong as you allow it to be. Whenever you experience a negative feeling, instead of focusing on it, get busy right away. If you're angry about something, cross something off your to-do list. If possible, do something that requires your full attention.
- **Interrupt:** Do something silly or unusual to break the pattern. Shout, do a silly dance or speak with a strange voice.
- **Move:** Stand up, go for a walk, do push-ups, dance, or use a power posture. By changing your physiology, you can change the way you feel.
- **Listen to music:** Listening to your favorite music may shift your emotional state.
- **Shout:** Talk to yourself with a loud and authoritarian voice and give yourself a pep talk. Use your voice and words to change your emotions.

B. Take action

- **Do it anyway:** Leave your feeling alone and do what you have to do. Mature adults do what they have to do whether they feel like it or not.
- **Do something about it:** Your behavior indirectly changes your feelings. Ask yourself, "What action can I take in today to change the way I feel?" Then, go do it.

C. Become aware of your emotions

- **Write it down:** Take a pen and paper and write down what you worry about, why, and what you can do about it. Be as specific as possible.
- **Write down what happened:** Take a piece of paper and write down what exactly happened to generate the negative emotion. Don't write down your interpretation of it or the drama you created around it. Write down the raw facts. Now ask yourself, in the grand scheme of your life, is it really that big a deal?
- **Talk:** Have a discussion with a friend. You may be overreacting, making things worse than they are. Sometimes, all you need is a different perspective.
- **Remember a time when you felt good about yourself:** This can help you get back in that state and gain a new perspective. Ask yourself the following questions, "How did it feel?" "What was I thinking at the time?" "What was my outlook on life at the time?"
- **Let your emotion go:** Ask yourself, "Can I let that emotion go?" Then, allow yourself to release it.
- **Allow your emotions to be:** Stop trying to resist your emotions or to change them. Allow them to be what they are.
- **Embrace your emotion:** Stay with your emotions. Look at them as closely as possible while doing your best to remain detached. Become curious about them. What are they exactly at their core?

D. Just relax

- **Rest:** Take a nap or a break. When you're tired, you're more likely to experience negative emotions than when you are properly rested.
- **Breathe:** Breathe slowly to relax. The way you breathe affects your emotional state. Use breathing techniques to calm you down, or to give you more energy.
- **Relax:** Take a few minutes to relax your muscles. Start by relaxing your jaw, the tension around your eyes and the muscles on your face. Your body affects your emotions. As you relax your body, your mind also relaxes.
- **Bless your problems:** Thank your problems. Understand they are here for a reason and will serve you in some way.

2. Long-term solutions

The following techniques will help you manage your negative emotions long-term.

A. Analyze your negative emotions

- **Identify the story behind your emotions:** Take a pen and paper, and write down all the reasons why you have these emotions in the first place. What assumptions do you hold? How did you interpret what's happening to you? Now, see if you can let go of this particular story.
- **Write down your emotions in a journal:** Take a few minutes each day to write down how you felt. Look for recurrent patterns. Then, use affirmations, visualization,

or a relevant exercise to help you overcome these emotions.

- **Practice mindfulness:** Observe your emotions throughout the day. Meditation will help you do this. Another way is simply to engage in an activity while being fully present. As you're doing this, observe what's going on in your mind.

B. Move away from negativity

- **Change environment:** If you're surrounded by negativity, change your environment. Move to a different place, or reduce the time you spend with negative friends.
- **Remove counterproductive activities:** Remove or reduce the time you spend on any activity not having a positive impact on your life. This could be reducing the time you spend watching TV or surfing the internet.

C. Condition your mind

- **Create daily rituals:** This will help you to experience more positive emotions. Meditate, exercise, repeat affirmations, create a gratitude journal, and so on. (The best time to deposit positive thoughts in your mind is right before going to sleep and first thing in the morning.)
- **Exercise:** Exercise regularly. Exercise improves your mood and is good for your emotional and physical health.

D. Increase your energy

The less energy you have, the more likely you are to experience negative emotions.

- **Improve your sleep:** Make sure you get enough sleep. If possible, go to bed and wake up at the same time every day.
- **Eat healthier food:** As the saying goes, "You are what you eat." Junk food will negatively impact your energy levels, so take steps to improve your diet.
- **Rest:** Take regular naps, or take a few minutes to relax
- **Breathe:** Learn to breathe properly.

E. Ask for help

- **Consult a professional:** if you have deep emotional issues such as extreme low self-esteem or depression, it might be wise to consult a professional.

4

———

PART IV. HOW TO USE YOUR EMOTIONS TO GROW

I suggest to you that every situation, every moment, provides the opportunity for self-growth and development of your character. Reality keeps bringing us circumstances—sometimes I picture them as waves breaking on the shore—and we have the chance to keep merging with that reality to fit ourselves to it, to dive into those waves.

— David K. Reynolds, author of Constructive Living.

We've seen what emotions are, how they are formed, and how you can reprogram your mind to experience more positive emotions. Now, let's see how you can use your emotions as a tool for personal growth.

Most people underestimate how useful emotions can be. They never truly realize they can use their emotions to grow.

Think of it this way. Your emotions send you a message. They tell you that your current interpretation of reality is biased. The problem is never reality, but the way you interpret it. Never forget, you have the power to find meaning and joy even in the worse situations.

For instance, Alice Sommer had every reason in the world to feel hopeless. She was imprisoned in a concentration camp during WWII and didn't know how long she had left to live. She, nevertheless, found joy. As she recalls:

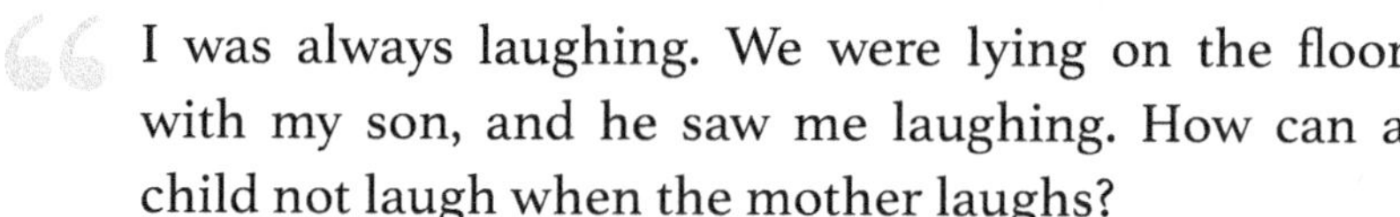

> I was always laughing. We were lying on the floor with my son, and he saw me laughing. How can a child not laugh when the mother laughs?

— ALICE SOMMER

Nick Vujicic believed he would never be happy. After all, he was born with no arms or legs. As he said in one of the lectures he gave at a school,

> What kind of husband am I gonna be if I can't even hold my wife's hand?

— NICK VUJICIC

Under these circumstances, nobody would have blamed him if he had remained bitter all his life. However, he overcame his challenges and today, in addition to being a successful motivational speaker, he's a happy husband and father of two.

These two examples show us we can overcome even the most challenging situations. They show us negative emotions don't last forever. Challenging times in our life are often the events that allow us to grow as human beings. Even a complete nervous breakdown can serve as a wake-up call for people.

In this section, you'll learn how emotions work and how you can use them to grow, while simultaneously reducing the emotional suffering they create.

To start using your emotions as a tool for your personal growth, make sure you complete the exercises in this section.

Record your emotions

Spend a couple of minutes each day to record how you feel and rate yourself on a scale of 1 to 10, one being the worse you could feel and ten being the best (refer to the 7-Day Mood Log at the end of this workbook).

Not being good enough

Identify triggers

What thought are you identifying with? Which areas of your life are concerned?

Write down the following:

Situations in which you feel like you aren't good enough

-

-

-

-

-

-

-

-

-

. . .

Thoughts you identify with (your story)

-

-

-

-

-

-

Overcoming the feeling of unworthiness

Keeping track of your accomplishments

Exercise 1 - Create a win log

Write down your daily accomplishments.

- Write down all the things you've accomplished in your
  life. Come up with a list of fifty things (See Win Log
  available at the end of this workbook).
- At the end of each day, write down all the things you've
  accomplished that day. (See 7-Day Mood Log)

Try to come up with 5 to 10 things each day.

Exercise 2 - Fill up your self-esteem jar

write down each thing you've accomplished on separate pieces of
paper and put them into a jar.

Exercise 3 - Create a positive journal

Write down every compliment you receive. Your colleague told you your shoes look nice, write it down. Your friend complimented your hair, write it down. Your boss told you you did a great job, write it down as well.

Learn to accept compliments

Exercise 1 - Accept compliments

This simple exercise is here to help you accept a compliment. Whenever someone compliments you, say the following:

Thank you *insert the person's name*.

No "Thank you, but...", "Thank you, you too" or "It wasn't a big deal", just "Thank you".

Exercise 2 - Appreciation game

The purpose of this game is to learn to appreciate things about yourself than you didn't previously acknowledge (or like). Tell your partner three things you appreciate about them and ask them to do the same. Be as specific as possible and don't worry about coming up with big things.

Below are some examples:

- I appreciate that you prepared breakfast this morning even though you were in a rush
- I appreciate that you picked up the kids today
- I appreciate the way you always listen to my problems after work

Getting defensive

Whenever you get defensive, ask yourself the following questions:

- What am I trying to protect here?
- Can I let go of that belief?
- What would I be without that belief?

Stress/Worry

Make a list of your major sources of stress

Write down what causes the most stress in your typical week. Come up with at least ten things.

-

-

-

-

-

-

-

-

-

-

-

·   ·   ·

Reframe the situation

Now, for each thing ask yourself the following questions:

- Is that situation stressful in itself?
- What would I need to believe in order to experience stress in that specific situation?
- What would I need to believe in order to reduce/remove stress in that particular situation?

Make a list of your worries

As you did with stressful situations, make a list of things (past or future) you worry about. You may end up writing similar things as in the previous examples and that's fine.

Examples of things you may worry about are your health, your financial situation, your work, your relationships or your family

Now, write ten things you're worrying about in a typical week.

	Worries	Level of control
#1		
#2		
#3		
#4		
#5		
#6		
#7		
#8		
#9		
#10		

Sort out your worries

- Look at your list of stressful situations. Put a C (control), a SC (Some control) or an NC (No control) next to each item in the table.
- Now, for things you have (some) control over, write down what you could do about it. What concrete actions could you take?

Change, reframe or eliminate stressful situations

Go over your list and look for things you have no control over. Write down below what you could do to change, reframe or eliminate these things. If you can't do anything, can you let go of your need to control them and, instead, accept them?

Things I have no control over (NC)	Can I change, reframe, eliminate or let these things go?

Caring what people think of you

Change your view of the way people perceive you

Exercise 1 - Realizing people don't care

This exercise will help you understand at a deeper level than most people are not really concern about you.

Write down the name of one person you know:

____

Write down how often you're thinking about that person in your day-to-day life:

____

____

____

____

Now, put yourself in the shoes of that person. How much do you think he or she thinks about you?

____

____

____

____

How much is he or she taking notes of what you do or say?

____

____

____

____

What do you think he or she is worrying about right now?

____

____

____

____

Repeat this process with at least two more people

Exercise 2 - Realizing that you do not care

- Go through your day and try to remember all the people you met or interacted with. It might the waitress in the restaurant you went to for lunch, people you saw on the street etc.
- Now ask yourself how much you thought about these people prior to this exercise.
- Acknowledge the fact you don't think of other people much neither do they. Let it sink and allow yourself to feel liberated

People you interacted with today	How much you thought about them

Stop being overly attached to your self-image

Write down below all the things you're afraid to be judged on. Maybe you worry about your look or you're afraid of saying something silly. Then, write down why you care:

Things I'm afraid to be judged on	Why I care

Resentment

4-step method to let go of resentment

1. Changing/reevaluating your interpretation

Write down what exactly happened. After you remove your interpretation, what are the hard facts?

____

____

____

____

2. Confronting the situation

If your resentment is directed toward people, perhaps, you need to have an honest discussion with them. If you can't talk to that person directly, you can write a letter. Even if you don't send it, the simple act of writing a letter may help you let go of some of your resentment.

3. Forgiving

Now, that you've found a channel to express yourself, you can forgive. Write down how your resentment affects your happiness and peace of mind:

____

____

____

____

Now, imagine how your life would be and how you would feel once you let go of resentment. Do it right now. Let go and allow yourself to forgive.

4. Forgetting

Finally, forget. Commit to letting go of thoughts of resentment. When such thoughts arise, let go of them.

Depression

Reconnect with your body and your emotions

Do one or several of the following things:

- **Exercise:** Exercising is a great way to calm your mind and connect with your body and has a positive effect on your mood.
- **Meditate:** Meditation is a great way to observe your mind and stop identifying with your thoughts so heavily.
- **Get busy:** Getting busy allows you to avoid excessive thinking.
- **Focus on other:** Dale Carnegie in his book How to Stop Worrying and Start Living, argues that depression can be cured in 14 days. How? Just by thinking of ways to help one person every day for two weeks.

Jealousy

Identify who you are jealous of

Write down who you are jealous of. Now, what does it say about you and what you want from life?

-

-

-

Cooperate rather than compete

Think of a time in the past when you felt jealous of someone else's accomplishments. Now, ask yourself why you felt that way. Then, ask yourself:

- What would supporting that person look like?
- How could I cooperate with the person?
- Why is that person's success good for me?

Compare apples to apples

Select someone you often compare yourself to. Write down all the things you're doing better than that person

Person I compare myself to:

____

Things I'm doing better:

-

-

-

-

-

-

-

Then, acknowledge how biased your initial comparison was.

Feel free to repeat this exercise with other people you compare yourself to.

Fear/Discomfort

Move out of your comfort zone

Answer the following question:

"What is the one thing that I know I should be doing, but that I have procrastinated on because of fear?".

____

____

____

____

Do that thing.

Every day do one thing that makes you uncomfortable (even just a little bit). Write down below, uncomfortable you could be doing every day:

-

-

-

-

-

-

Procrastination

How to Crush Procrastination in 16 Simple Steps

1. Understand what's hidden behind procrastination.

Make sure you identify all the reasons behind procrastination and be honest with yourself. If you lack motivation, ask yourself why.

2. Remind yourself of the cost of procrastination

Procrastination is not a minor issue. Its cost is both direct and indirect:

- The direct consequence of procrastination is that you'll achieve far less than you could during your time spent on earth.
- The indirect consequence of procrastination is that you may feel bad about yourself.

Write down what procrastination costs you. How does it affect your peace of mind? Your self-esteem? Your ability to achieve your dreams?

-

-

-

-

. . .

3. Uncover your story

Write down all your excuses. Then, address them one by one. (examples: I don't have time, I'm too old, I'm not smart enough, I'm too tired etc.)

Excuses	Counterarguments

4. Rewrite your story

Look at your excuses. Now that you've identified your story, create a new more empowering story to neutralize your old excuses. See examples below:

- I don't have time for that → I find and make time for whatever I'm committed to.
- I'm too tired → I have control over my mind and I have more energy than I think. When I schedule a task I complete it.

Create affirmations or mantras around your new story. Repeat them to yourself every morning and throughout the day until they become part of your identity.

· · ·

Your affirmation(s):

-

-

-

5. Clarify your why

Look at one important task you regularly procrastinate on. Why is that? Write down how you can make these tasks part of your vision:

____

____

____

____

6. Identify the ways you distract yourself

What are your own ways to procrastinate on that important task?

Examples: going for a walk, watching videos on Youtube, checking Facebook etc.

How I procrastinate:

____

____

____

____

7. Stay with the urge

As you feel the urge to *insert your distraction here*, stay with the emotion. How do you feel? Allow yourself to feel that emotion. Don't judge yourself. Don't blame yourself. Just accept what is. As you do so, you'll gain more control of your mind.

8. Record everything you do

Record everything you do for a week. Then, see how much time you spend doing unproductive activities (you can use the Time Log sheet at the end of this workbook)

9. Set a clear intent behind everything you do

Before working on a task, make sure you know exactly what needs to be done. Ask yourself, what am I trying to accomplish here?

10. Prepare your environment

Your mind doesn't like what's hard. It wants things to be easy. Thus, make sure you can start working on your task immediately by removing any friction or obstacle.

Write down below what you can do to make it easier to work on your important task:

____

____

____

____

11. Start small

Making your tasks smaller will help you overcome procrastination. Not only that, but it will also allow you to build momentum.

Chunk down your important task:

12. Create quick wins

Set small goals every day and accomplish them consistently for a few weeks. As you do that you'll increase your self-esteem and be better equipped to complete more challenging tasks in the future.

Write quick wins for your task(s) (select 1 to 3 tasks)

-

-

-

13. Just get started

Often, when you start working on a task, you'll enter what is called 'the flow' and things become effortless. Look at the quick wins you wrote down previously and take a few seconds to commit to getting started on these tasks.

. . .

14. Create daily habits to support you

If you tend to procrastinate on important tasks, commit to working on them first thing in the morning. Write down one task you will work on first thing in the morning.

My one task:

15. Use visualization

You can also use visualization to help you overcome procrastination. Below are two specific ways you can do so:

1. Visualizing yourself doing the task: Before you start a task, visualize yourself working on it.

2. Visualizing yourself having completed the task: Imagine yourself having completed the task. How would you feel once the task is done? Liberated? Happy? Proud?

Additional tip:

Each time you finish a challenging task, take a few seconds to notice how that makes you feel. Remind yourself of that feeling whenever you start working on a difficult task.

16. Build accountability

How can you build accountability for your important tasks and goals (examples: have an accountability partner, hire a coach, send your list of goals to a friend every week etc.)

Lack of motivation

Creating a system

To help you take action when you lack motivation it is important to:

- Have a system that allows you to stay on track with your goals
- Build the self-discipline needed to do things when you don't feel like it
- Have self-compassion and love yourself instead of blaming yourself

What daily routine can you put in place to stay on track with your goals? (examples: create a morning ritual with positive affirmations, visualizations or work on your most important task first thing in the morning)

____

____

____

____

To build self-discipline, what task can you commit to doing every day for the next 30 days?

My tasks:

-

-

. . .

What words of encouragement or mantras can you use to encourage yourself when you feel down?

7-Day Mood Log

Record how you feel each day and rate yourself on a scale of 1 to 10, 1 being the worse you could feel and 10 being the best. In addition, acknowledge your small daily accomplishments.

Day 1

How did I feel today?

0 ____ 10

What did you accomplish today?

-

-

-

-

-

Remarks (if any):

Day 2

How did I feel today?

<pre>0   10</pre>

What did you accomplish today?

-

-

-

-

-

Remarks (if any):

Day 3

How did I feel today?

<u>0</u>____<u>10</u>

What did you accomplish today?

-

-

-

-

-

Remarks (if any):

Day 4

How did I feel today?

0 ____ 10

What did you accomplish today?

-

-

-

-

-

Remarks (if any):

Day 5

How did I feel today?

0 ____ 10

What did you accomplish today?

-

-

-

-

-

Remarks (if any):

How did I feel today?

0 ————————————————————————————————————— 10

What did you accomplish today?

-

-

-

-

-

Remarks (if any):

Day 7

How did I feel today?

0 ____ 10

What did you accomplish today?

-

-

-

-

-

Remarks (if any):

Now, answer the questions below to help better understand your negative emotions and how you feed them often unconsciously.

What negative emotions did you experience?

____

____

____

____

What caused these emotions? (Did specific thoughts/external events lead you to feel the way?)

____

____

____

____

What really happened?

____

____

____

____

What was your interpretation of what happened?

What would you need to believe to feel that way?

Are your beliefs true?

If you had interpreted thoughts or events differently, could you have felt better?

____

____

____

____

How did you get back to your neutral state?

____

____

____

____

What happened exactly? (Did you change your thoughts, take action or did it happen naturally?)

____

____

____

____

What could you have done to avoid or reduce these negative emotions?

Win Log

Write down below everything you've accomplished in your life. Aim at 50 things or more.

1.

2.

3.

4.

5.

6.

7.

8.

9.

10.

11.

12.

13.

14.

15.

16.

17.

18.

19.

20.

21.

22.

23.

24.

25.

26.

27.

28.

29.

30.

31.

32.

33.

34.

35.

36.

37.

38.

39.

40.

41.

42.

43.

44.

45.

46.

47.

48.

49.

50.

Time Log

71

Day 1	Day 2	Day 3	Day 4

Time Log

Day 5	Day 6	Day 7

NOTES (if any)

73

MASTER YOUR
MOTIVATION WORKBOOK

Stop —Do that one thing now!

Complete one task you've been putting off for a long time. And complete it now!

Ask yourself the following questions:

- What is the one task I know I should do but don't want to do?
- What one task, if I were to do right now, would free my mind the most?

PART I

ASSESS YOUR SITUATION

1. Accept your situation

Accept your current situation completely and show yourself compassion. Let go of any sense of guilt and remove the weight on your shoulder. It's time for a fresh beginning.

2. State the facts

Write down the raw facts regarding your current situation. Look at your situation objectively. What exactly happened?

What happened:

____

____

____

____

____

____

____

____

____

____

Then, ask yourself the following questions:

Will that even matter twenty years from now?

____

Is it the first time I feel that way?

____

Is it really that big of a deal?

____

Is that event relevant on the world scale?

____

What can I do about it now?

____

____

____

____

____

3. Find an external perspective

Seek an external perspective by doing one (or several) of the following:

a. Talk to a friend

Who could I talk to?

____

When will I talk to that friend?

____

b. See your situation from someone else's eyes

Who would that person be?

____

What would they think?

____

____

____

____

____

____

c. Imagine your best friend being in a similar situation.

What would your best friend think?

____

____

____

____

____

What would you tell them? How would you support them?

____

____

____

____

____

PART II

BUILD MOMENTUM

1. Declutter

A. Reconnect with the present

Meditate on the fact that this moment is the only thing that will ever exist. The past is gone and the future has yet to come.

Write down any insight/thought below:

____

____

____

____

____

____

Transfer responsibility to your future you

Go through the three-step process below:

1. Take a few deep breaths and relax
2. Remember any past accomplishments and challenges you've overcome in the past. You've been able to survive up until now so your future self will do just fine. Imagine yourself transferring all your worries about your future to your future self. Feel yourself become lighter and more present (you can write down all your accomplishment using the win log at the end of this workbook).
3. Refocus on what you can do today and only on that.

Write down below what you can do today:

____

____

____

____

____

____

B. Sort out your worries

Fill in the table below:

What I worry about	Level of control (C/NC/SC)	How it benefits me	What I can do about it

C. Close open loops

Write down every task present in the back of your mind. Then, schedule time to complete these tasks.

Things to do:

-

-

-

-

-

-

-

-

-

-

-

-

-

-

-

-

D. Free up your schedule

Identify why you're not saying no

Fill in the table below:

Things I said yes to	Y/N (wanted to say yes or no?)	Why I couldn't say no

How to say no

a) Start small

What small favor(s) or invitation(s) could you say no to?

-

-

-

-

b) Stop over justifying yourself What will you say to decline the invitation(s)

Example:

- I'm sorry but parties are not my things so I'm going to skip this time.
- I'm sorry but right now I'm entirely focused on a very important project.

Write down below what you could say to decline invitation(s):

____

____

____

____

____

____

c) Practice saying no

Visualize a particular situation and see yourself saying no. What words would you use? How would you say them?

____

____

____

____

____

____

d) Offer alternatives

In the future, what alternative(s) could you offer instead of just saying yes or no? Write a few of them below:

-

-

-

-

-

Eliminate unpleasant tasks

Fill in the table below:

Your unpleasant tasks	What can you do about them (delegate them? Eliminate them? Reframe them?)

E. Declutter your desk

Remove anything necessary on your desk such as files you don't need right now, your smartphone etc.

F. Declutter your physical environment

Get rid of *everything* that you don't need to only keep things that bring your joy

1. Sort out your possession by categories (clothes, books, papers, miscellany and items with sentimental values)
2. Gather all the items in the first category, put the unnecessary ones in a plastic bag.
3. Move on to the next category and repeat the same process

G. Revise your forecast

When you set your daily goals, double the time you think you need to complete each of your tasks and see what happens.

H. Take breaks

Test one of the following techniques for a week:

1. Taking breaks every 75-90 minutes (with 10 to 15-minute breaks)
2. Taking breaks every 52 minutes (with 17-minute breaks)
3. Taking break every 25 minutes (with 5-minute breaks)

Which technique will you test in the next seven days?

____

2. Focus

A. Assess your productivity

Create your time log using the time log table at the end of this
workbook.

B. Leverage the 80/20 Principle

What are the 20% of your tasks that bring you 80% of your results?

For each of the areas below, write down the few things that if you
were to do, would make a big difference.

Social life:

-

-

-

Finance

-

-

-

Health

-

-

-

Well-being

-

-

-

C. Destroy distraction

What one thing could you do right now to boost your motivation? If you feel any resistance, seek to identify the root of that resistance (fear of not being good enough, lack of clarity, lack of interest or lack of energy)

One thing I could do to boost my motivation is:

____

____

____

____

____

D. Optimize your environment

What could you change in your environment to feel more motivated and make it more likely you achieve your life goals?

What physical objects could add or remove?

____

____

____

____

Who could stop seeing or start hanging out with?

____

____

____

____

What changes could you make at home on at your workplace?

____

____

____

____

Other ways you will optimize your environment:

____

____

____

____

Digital detox

Experiment with full and partial detox:

Full detox: for 24 hours, 48 hours or more, refrain from using any digital device.

When will you start your full detox?

____

Partial detox: create your own rules regarding your digital environment. For the next seven days, do your best to follow these rules you set and see how you feel.

When you will do with your seven-day partial detox?

____

3. Reignite

A. Do more of what you love

Let go of what doesn't make you happy

Make a list of what you do every day. Then, ask yourself, "what are the activities that fail to bring me the sense of fulfillment I'm looking for?"

Activity	Level of fulfillment

Identify what you love to do

Answer the following questions:

When was the last time you had a great day and why? What did you do?

What are you looking forward to the most every day?

If you could do only one activity you love every day, what would that be?

What activities, if you did, would allow you to feel good at the end of your day?

____

____

____

____

____

How would you describe your ideal day to your best friend?

____

____

____

____

____

Is there something you enjoyed doing in the past but stopped doing?

____

Is there something you've always wanted to try but never muster the courage to?

____

Write down 20 things you love to do:

1.

2.

3.

4.

5.

6.

7.

8.

9.

10.

11.

12.

13.

14.

15.

16.

17.

18.

19.

20.

B. Identify what really motivates you

Identify what you really want

Ask yourself the following questions:

Is it really my goal or is it someone else's goal?

____

____

____

____

Is it exciting me? Do I feel pulled by it or do I have to continuously push and struggle?

____

____

____

____

What will I gain from achieving that goal? And is it what I want? Will it really improve my life?

____

____

____

____

Find your strengths

Answer the following questions:

What are your biggest strengths?

____

____

____

____

What is it that you believe only you can do? What is unique about you?

____

____

____

____

What do you find so easy to do that you genuinely don't understand why others have difficulties doing it?

____

____

____

____

What people compliment you on? If you don't know, ask your friends, family members or colleagues

____

____

____

____

If you need help to find your strengths, check out my free ebook *Find What You Love* at the URL below:

https://whatispersonaldevelopment.org/find-what-you-love

Identify your core values

Fill in the table below:

	Top 5 core values	Living by then? (Y/N)	How could I better align with them?
#1			
#2			
#3			
#4			
#5			

Understanding your personality

Take the following test to help you better understand your personality.

Introversion test:

https://www.quietrev.com/the-introvert-test/

Briggs Myers's test (16 personalities):

http://www.humanmetrics.com/cgi-win/jtypes2.asp

Big Five Personality test:

https://www.truity.com/test/big-five-personality-test

Now, what one thing could you do to better express your personality?

Identifying your core values

Creating your vision

Write down your answer to the following questions:

a) How do you want the world to change as the result of your own actions?

b) What group of people, causes or organizations do you want to serve in this world?

____

____

____

____

c) If you could solve only one problem in the world, what would that be? Why?

____

____

____

____

d) What is your unique ways to express yourself to this world? What verbs best describe

____

____

____

____

C. Set exciting goals

a) Reconnecting with your original whys

Take some time to reconnect with your vision. Look at different areas one by one and ask yourself whether you're moving in the right direction. Observe the gap between where you are and what you aspire for.

Career:

Why did you choose your current career? What were your aspirations when you first got started? What motivated you?

____

____

____

____

____

____

Family:

What original vision did you have for you and your family? How could you close the gap between your csituation and what you aspire for?

____

____

____

____

____

____

Relationship:

How did you feel at the beginning of your relationships? What were you deepest aspirations

____

____

____

____

____

Social life:

What the ideal social life for you? What could you do to move closer to this ideal?

____

____

____

____

____

____

b) Make new plans

Write down your answers to the following questions: what do I want?

Let your imagination go wild and make sure you pay attention to any sign of excitement you may experience.

Is there any goal or idea you feel drawn toward?

____

____

____

____

____

Is there anything that makes you feel really good?

____

____

____

____

____

Is there something you feel like doing right now or can't wait to make happen in the near future?

____

____

____

____

____

Remember that how you feel is important. Your emotions tell you a lot about yourself and what you value the most.

c) Strengthening your why

Answer the question, "What's the most important (and exciting) goal I want to pursue right now?

Now, what are all the reasons it must happen?"

Come up with a list of at least twenty reasons you want to achieve that goal. If you can, try to come up with 100 reasons.

20 reasons it must happen:

1.

2.

3.

4.

5.

6.

7.

8.

9.

10.

11.

12.

13.

14.

15.

16.

17.

18.

19.

20.

4. Jump

A. Do the impossible

Write down everything you think you could never do. Now, select one thing in your list and commit to doing it this week or this month.

What I think I could never do

-

-

-

-

-

-

-

-

-

The one "impossible" thing I will do:

____

B. Meet new people

Answer the following questions:

What type of people do I want to meet? And what are their values, vision, traits of character etc.)

Where can I find them?

What concrete actions will I do to meet like-minded people?

____

____

____

____

____

C. Break old patterns

How do you think, feel and act now as opposed to before?

Remember a time you felt motivated. What were you thinking, feeling and doing? Spend a few minutes reconnecting with the way you felt.

	Before	Now
How I feel		
How I think		
How I act		

Do thing differently

What different activities could you engage in now? Write them
down below:

-

-

-

-

-

D. Perform an act of kindness

Do one act of kindness today.

Your act of kindness:

____

5. Complete

A. Complete tasks one hundred percent

Write down below some unfinished projects.

-

-

-

-

How does that make you feel?

____

____

____

____

Now, remember a time you completed a project that was important to you.

How did you feel? And what happened after that? Did you feel more motivated? More confident? Write your answer below:

____

____

____

____

B. Destroy shiny object syndrome

Overcome distractions using the following steps:

- **Be aware:** See which area of your life you fall off track with your goals. Understand how success works and change your mindset accordingly.

- **Implement an effective strategy**: Spend time to craft an effective plan that, when you follow, will deliver the results you want. Don't reinvent the wheel. Instead, copy what people who've achieved your goal did.
- **Be patient:** Life is a marathon, not a sprint. Think long-term and you will do better than most people. Your mantras: "Be patient" and "it's okay you have time".
- **Be consistent:** Stay focus on a specific course of action and do that consistently every day until you achieve the results you want.
- **Overcome your fears:** be honest with yourself and face your fears instead of using procrastination as a way to stay within your comfort zone. Remember: action cures fear.
- **Commit:** Set a specific goal that excites you, establish a clear deadline and resolve to achieve that goal. Make it public or find an accountability partner or coach if needed.
- **Avoid information overload:** have a clear intent behind what you do, create a learning schedule and remove as many external stimuli as you possibly can. The more deliberate you are, the less overwhelmed you will feel.

C. Honor your promises

a) Keep your promises to others

What are some of the things you said to people you would do but haven't?

-

-

-

-

Do one of these things now.

The one thing you'll do:

____

b) Keep your promises to yourself

For a week, set 3 simple daily tasks and complete them. Write down below the 3 daily tasks you'll complete for seven days:

1.

2.

3.

D. Procrastinate smartly

Write down all the small actions you could take right now. Try to lean towards activities you enjoy or at least, activities that move you in the right direction.

-

-

-

-

-

-

-

-

-

Now, select one action and resolve to take it now or, if you can't, later today.

Your one action:

____

E. Deep dive

Identify one project you've started but haven't completed. Then, give yourself a short period of time to focus on it until it's complete one hundred percent.

One project you haven't completed:

____

When you will complete it:

____

PART III

SUSTAIN MOMENTUM

1. Acknowledge

A. Complete three tasks

Write down three tasks you want to complete today, finish them and celebrate your wins. Repeat the process every day until it becomes a habit.

Today's three tasks:

1.

2.

3.

B. Feel proud of yourself

Find something you're proud of and acknowledge yourself for that now. Say to yourself "I'm proud of you for *insert what makes you proud of yourself*."

I'm proud of myself for:

Then, before going to bed, think of three things you're proud of.

C. Right actions vs. right results

Look at goals you want to accomplish in various areas of your life. Identify the right actions for each of them. What are a few things that if you keep doing repeatedly would allow you to build momentum over time and eventually achieve your goals?

Goal #1

Right actions:

-

-

-

Goal #2

Right actions:

-

-

-

Goal #3

Right actions:

-

-

-

2. Commit

A. Seek external accountability

What is one thing you could do to build accountability? Write it down below:

____

B. Create a morning ritual

Create your personalized morning ritual using the steps below:

1. Clarifying your "why". Write down your main objective below (feeling grateful, being more productive etc.)

____

____

____

____

2. Getting excited. Write down one or several activities you thoroughly enjoy and want to do first thing in the morning.

____

____

____

____

3. Identifying obstacles and preparing yourself mentally. Write down potential obstacles and visualize yourself dealing with them.

----

4. Selecting the components of your morning ritual. Select activities that will feed your body, mind and soul. Write them down below

----

----

5. Deciding how much time you have available. Write down how much time you will dedicate to your morning ritual

----

----

6. Removing roadblocks and distractions. Write down what you will do to remove frictions. (Prepare your running gears the day before etc.)

____

____

____

____

7. Setting yourself up for success. What will you do to make sure you get enough sleep so that you wake up energized and stick to your morning ritual?

____

____

____

____

8. Committing one hundred percent. Spend a moment to really commit to doing it.

9. Undertaking the 30-Day Challenge. Commit to sticking to your new morning ritual for 30 days. Write down below what morning ritual you commit to.

I commit to:

____

C. Live with intent

Set daily intents using the step-by-step method below.

1. Write down the main segments of your day below (i.e, going to work, eating lunch etc.):

-

-

-

-

-

-

-

-

-

-

-

2. Select the segment(s) in which you want to feel different than you currently do.

-

-

. . .

3. Set a specific trigger for your intent. Write down your trigger below:

____

4. Decide what you will do to change your emotional state. Create a sort of ritual before you enter that segment of your day. Write it down below:

____

____

____

____

5. Set reminders. If necessary, have something that reminds you of the intended action (post-it, timer etc.)

My reminder(s) are:

____

____

____

____

D. Commit to 30-day challenges

Implementing a 30-day challenge is a great way to build momentum and boost your motivation. Below is what you can do to make your 30-day challenge a success.

How to undertake a 30-Day Challenge successfully

Answer the following questions.

a) What would make the biggest impact on your life if you committed to start or stop doing it for thirty days?

———————————————————————————————

———————————————————————————————

———————————————————————————————

———————————————————————————————

b) What exactly do you commit to doing every day for the next thirty days?

———————————————————————————————

———————————————————————————————

———————————————————————————————

———————————————————————————————

c) How will you create accountability for your challenge? (who will be your accountability, how will you communicate and how often etc.

d) What will happen if you fail? (What are the consequences of not following through?)

e) How will you reward yourself?

E. Change your self-talk

Think of something you believe you can't do well. For instance, "I can't talk in front of an audience".

Then, replace the expression "I can't" with each of the expressions below.

- I can do/become...
- I will do/become...
- I want to do/become...
- I love doing/becoming...
- I choose to do/become...
- What if I could do/become...?
- Imagine if I could do/become...? How can I do/become...?
- What would I need to believe to be able to do/become...?
- How would it make me feel if I could do/become...?

Your turn now:

I can

____

I will

____

I want to

____

I love

____

I choose to

____

What if I could

____

Imagine if I could

____

How can I

____

What would I need to believe to be able to

____

How would I make me feel if I could

____

F. Develop self-compassion

Undertake a 7-day compassion challenge. For the next seven days, wherever possible, refrain from criticizing yourself. To help you become aware of your negative self-talk, I encourage you to wear a rubber band around your wrist and to snap it whenever you notice any self-criticism. Then, give yourself words of encouragement. They could be something like:

- "I know you're struggling right now, but you're doing the best you can."
- "You're doing okay. Everybody goes through challenging times once in a while."
- "I'm proud of you. Even though you feel the urge to criticize yourself, you still make an effort to be kinder to yourself."

Don't get too caught up with the exact words you should use. Your intention to be gentle with yourself is what matters the most. Over time, you'll find the right words to encourage yourself and show yourself the compassion you deserve.

G. Practice daily gratitude

Practice one of the exercises below for at least 7 days:

a) Thank people

Sit down on a chair or lie down in your bed and close your eyes. Then, think of someone you know and thank him or her. It doesn't matter who the person is. Whenever possible, think of something specific they did for you. Perhaps, they gave you some advice, helped you learn an important lesson or brought you joy during the time you spent with them. Repeat the process.

b) Thank items in your life

Select one specific item in the room you're sitting in right now. For instance, it could be your desk or the chair you're sitting in. Then, take the time to appreciate it.

- Think of the way this item improves your life.
- Think of all the people involved in its creation.

c) Create a gratitude journal

Buy a journal and every time you receive a compliment, write it down in your journal.

d) Gratitude exercise

Every day when you wake, write down three new things you would like to acknowledge. Try to come up with three different things each morning.

e) Gratitude meditation

Listen to gratitude meditation and follow the instructions. You'll find many examples on YouTube.

The one gratitude exercise I will experiment with is:

PART IV

25 SIMPLE STRATEGIES TO GET YOUR MOTIVATION BACK

Motivation comes and goes but they are many things you can do to get your motivation back. Below are some techniques you can use to get out of a slump and start generating momentum:

A. Get it done

Use the completion principle to get your motivation back.

1. Complete a task you've been putting off for too long. Identify one task or project you've been putting off for a while and go complete it right now.

2. Write it down, get it done. Write down a list of all things you know you have to do but have been putting off. Now, schedule a block of time to complete them by batching them together.

3. Complete a simple and easy task. Work on a small task that moves you toward your goal. Then, if you feel like it, work on another one and see where it leads you.

4. Complete one specific project. Deep dive on a specific project you have left unfinished and complete it one hundred percent.

5. Complete three things today. Write down three simple tasks you want to complete today. Complete them, then cross them off your list and say to yourself "good job!". Reward yourself with your favorite treat or movie at the end of the day. Repeat this process tomorrow and the day after.

B. Give yourself a break

Take a step back and get out of your head. Things probably aren't as bad as you think.

6. Look at the facts. Take a step back and look at your current situation from a purely objective point of view. What are the facts?

Facts are no big deal but your interpretation can be. Will you remember your current situation twenty years from now? Is that really a big deal? If not, can you let go?

7. Talk to a friend. Call a friend or meet him or her to get a different perspective.

8. Hire a coach or find an accountability partner. Find someone you can work with. It will give you a new perspective and will create accountability making it more likely you take consistent actions.

9. Take a break. Perhaps, all you need is a break. Take your day off. Have a relaxing weekend and just do nothing.

10. Cultivate self-compassion. Give yourself a break. How you feel now is fine. Just let go of self-criticism and encourage yourself instead.

11. Do something for someone else. Helping other people prevent you from being overly focused on yourself and on your own problem. Who could you help today? Could you buy a gift for someone? Could you send a thank you letter? Could you help someone with his or her goals?

12. Exercise. Get your body moving. Go for a run. Work out. Do yoga. Exercise is a great way to get out of your mind and into your body.

C. Sort things out

Put some order in your life. Too much clutter can make you feel stuck.

13. Sort out your worries. Make a list of all the things you worry about. Next to each item write down whether you have control (C), some control (SC) or no control (C) over these things. Practice letting go of things you have no control over. For things you have (some) control over, write down what you can do about it.

14. Free up your schedule. Be ruthless with the way you use your time. Seek to remove any activities you don't enjoy or that don't move you toward your ideal vision.

15. Declutter your desk. A cluttered desk can be the manifestation of a cluttered mind. Clean your desk and your computer. Reorganize files on your computer.

16. Declutter your digital space. Clean up your email box, unsubscribe from newsletters, remove softwares you don't use etc.

17. Declutter your house. Spend your weekend decluttering your house. Only keep things you love and remove anything else. (See declutter your physical environment)

D. Get the excitement back

Focus on what you love and do right and get your motivation back.

18. De more of what you love. Schedule time during your day to do one of the things you love the most.

19. Ask yourself what excites you. Sit at your desk, take a pen and a piece of paper and write down "What do I love?". Then, write anything that comes to mind. See what projects, goals or ideas you feel drawn toward.

20. Start a new exciting challenge. Forget about your small goals. Think of a challenge that really excites you no matter how big or unrealistic it may seem. Then, take one action that move you forward whether it is buying a book, watching a video or contacting someone.

21. Celebrate your accomplishments. Take a piece of paper and write down everything you've ever accomplished in your life. Make sure you acknowledge yourself for personal problems you overcome. The more specific, the better.

22. Express gratitude. Cultivate the habits of expressing gratitude for all the things you have going on for you. Focus on the positive.

E. Reinvent yourself

Do something different. You can't do the same thing and expect different results.

23. Move beyond your comfort zone. Go do something a little bit scary. Do something you've never done before. Is there anything you've always wanted to try but never dare to? Go do that.

24. Meet new people. Who do you want to be surrounded with? Find a group of like-minded people and join it (use Meetup.com for instance). Or create your own group to attract people you want to meet.

25. Break old patterns. Spend your day doing things you don't normally do. Call an old friend, go for a walk etc.

Win Log

Write down below everything you've accomplished in your life. Aim at 50 things or more.

1.

2.

3.

4.

5.

6.

7.

8.

9.

10.

11.

12.

13.

14.

15.

16.

17.

18.

19.

20.

21.

22.

23.

24.

25.

26.

27.

28.

29.

30.

31.

32.

33.

34.

35.

36.

37.

38.

39.

40.

41.

42.

43.

44.

45.

46.

47.

48.

49.

50.

Time Log

Day 1	Day 2	Day 3	Day 4

Time Log

Day 5	Day 6	Day 7
	150	

NOTES:

www.ingramcontent.com/pod-product-compliance
Lightning Source LLC
Chambersburg PA
CBHW071435130726
47997CB00006B/2096